HOPSCOTCH
STORIES OF
RELIGION

The Prince and Holika the Witch

First published in 2008 by
Franklin Watts
338 Euston Road
London
NW1 3BH

Franklin Watts Australia
Level 17/207 Kent Street
Sydney
NSW 2000

A CIP catalogue record for this book is available
from the British Library.

ISBN 978 0 7496 8371 9 (hbk)
ISBN 978 0 7496 8377 1 (pbk)

Series Editor: Melanie Palmer
Series Advisor: Dr Barrie Wade
Series Designer: Peter Scoulding

Printed in China

Franklin Watts is a division of
Hachette Children's Books,
an Hachette Livre UK company.
www.hachettelivre.co.uk

The Prince and Holika the Witch

by Anita Ganeri and David Lopez

FRANKLIN WATTS
LONDON • SYDNEY

About this book

The story of the Prince and Holika the Witch comes from the religion of Hinduism. Hinduism began at least 4,500 years ago in north-west India. Stories play an important part in Hinduism. They help to teach people about their faith in a way that is easy to understand. From an early age, Hindu children read and listen to stories about the gods and goddesses, and about events in the Hindu year. *The Prince and Holika the Witch* is associated with the great festival of Holi, which takes place in February or March each year to celebrate the coming of spring.

Once there was a demon king
called Hiran-yaka-shipu.
He lived in a beautiful palace.

King Hiran-yaka-shipu was very rich and powerful. But he was also greedy and cruel.

He thought that he was a god and wanted everyone to worship him.

The king had a son called Prahlad.
Unlike his wicked father, Prahlad
was gentle and kind.

Prince Prahlad knew his father was not a god. He worshipped Lord Vishnu instead.

The king was furious. His face
turned red with rage. He decided
to punish Prahlad.

"Take this foolish boy away!"

he shouted to his soldiers.

"Throw him off a cliff!"

The soldiers took Prahlad away
and threw him off the top of a
very high cliff.

But Lord Vishnu was watching over Prahlad and he floated gently to the ground, light as a feather.

When the soldiers brought Prahlad back, the king could not believe his eyes.

"Throw him into a pit of
poisonous snakes," he cried.
"See how he likes that!"

The soldiers threw Prahlad into a pit of snakes. But none of the snakes would bite him.

Instead, the snakes wrapped their long bodies around him and let him stroke their smooth heads.

When the king saw that Prahlad
was still alive and safe, he almost
exploded with rage.

18

"I don't care how you do it,"
he screamed at the soldiers.
"Just get rid of him!"

19

So the soldiers took Prahlad away and threw him in front of a charging elephant.

But the elephant did not hurt him. Instead, it stopped and bowed down in front of him.

In a terrible temper, the king
stormed off to see his sister,
a wicked witch called Holika.

"That boy needs teaching a lesson," Holika cackled. "Don't worry, I've got a cunning plan."

Next day, Holika lit a huge bonfire in the palace garden. Then she called for Prahlad.

"Let's play a game," she said.
"Hold my hand and we'll walk
into the fire."

"Don't worry about getting burned," she told Prahlad. "My magic powers will protect us."

But really wicked Holika planned
to leave Prahlad in the fire, while
she walked out safely.

Luckily, as so many times before,
Lord Vishnu was watching
over Prahlad.

Quick as a flash, he pulled
Prahlad from the flames and left
Holika to die instead.

Today people celebrate the great festival of Holi by lighting bright, blazing bonfires.

It reminds them of the story of Holika, the wicked witch and Prahlad, the gentle prince.

Hopscotch has been specially designed to fit the requirements of the Literacy Framework. It offers real books by top authors and illustrators for children developing their reading skills.

For more details go to:
www.franklinwatts.co.uk

* hardback